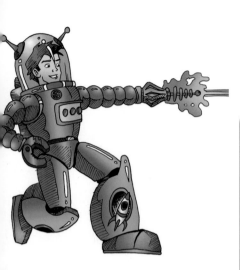

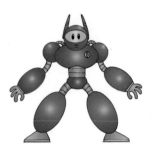

Welcome to **How To Draw Animals.** We all know that pictures can look really intimidating to attempt. They can seem complicated or difficult, and it is sometimes hard to even know where to start. The great thing about this book, though, is that it breaks down even the most detailed pictures into easily understandable steps, so you can start drawing almost right away.

We all know that drawing is a creative pastime, but people don't always realize that it's technical too. Don't let that put you off though. What it means is that pictures are constructed from various geometrical shapes, and it's possible, with practice, to train yourself to spot these shapes easily. For example, a person's head is shaped very much like an upside-down egg. This and many other secrets are all revealed in this book, so you'll become an expert in no time at all.

The main thing to remember is to have fun, and lots of it! Drawing different characters and scenes is really exciting, and all you need to begin with is a pencil and a sheet of paper.

There are thousands of different animals and creatures on our planet, and all of them are interesting and individual in their own way. Some animals display vivid, bright colors on their bodies. Others have armor-plating to protect them from predators. And then there are those that are the actual predators!

This book takes a small selection of animals and "critters," and explains how to draw them in easy-to-follow steps. Also, to make it easier for you to search for what you want to draw, the animals are grouped together with others of a similar species. These groups are:

Creepy crawlies: Spider, scorpion, dragonfly, butterfly
Sea-life: Fish, dolphin, shark, crab, seahorse
Birds: Parrot, penguin, American bald eagle
Domestic pets: Dog, cat, rabbit
Farm animals: Sheep, pig, horse, cow, rooster
Zoo animals: Lion, panda, giraffe, elephant
Reptiles & Amphibians: Snake, frog, gecko, crocodile

Many of the animals in this book are crazy cartoons that are great fun to draw and to color. But beware—some of these guys are more realistic, so don't get too close or they may bite!

So grab your pencil and paper, see what catches your eye, and get creating your own animal menagerie—because this chapter is wild!

HOW TO DRAW A SPIDER

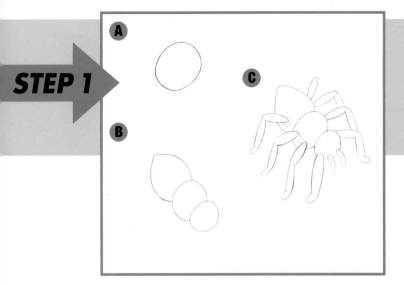

STEP 1

A The first stage of creating a gruesome tarantula is to sketch a large circle in the center of your page. This will be for the spider's thorax.

B Draw a smaller circle in front of this, which will form the head of your spider. Next, draw a fat teardrop shape behind the thorax, which is the tarantula's abdomen.

C Your spider's legs are constructed using long oval shapes. Its feet are tiny ovals that are the same width as the rest of the legs but set at an angle. The spider also has two small "feelers" on its head. These are constructed in the same way as its legs.

D Tarantulas have striped fur on their legs and body. The legs are candy-striped at the knees, feet, and where they join the body. There is also a large, pointed stripe running down the thorax onto the abdomen. Spiders have many eyes, so draw these on its head.

E In the final stage of pencil sketching, alter anything you aren't happy with before giving your spider an all-over "fuzzy" look. Do this with short, spiky pencil strokes.

Draw over all of the pencil lines that you're happy with using a black pen before erasing the leftover pencil lines. Your spider is now ready to color.

G Your tarantula should be a deep gray or black color, with orange stripes on its legs and a large white stripe on its back. Give it deep green eyes, and you have one seriously creepy crawly!

2

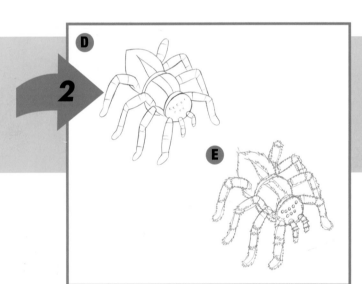

3

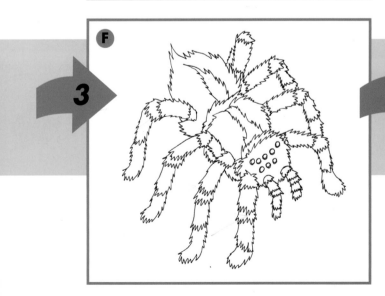

4

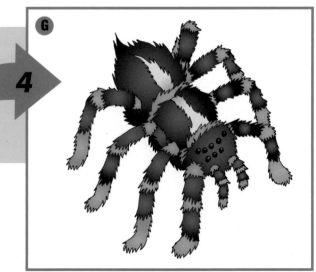

STEP 1

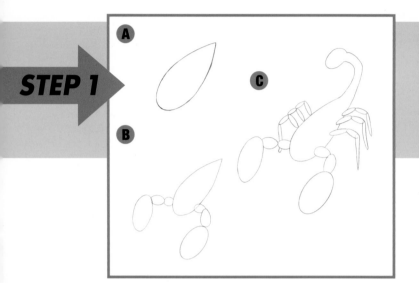

Ⓐ The main body of your scorpion is teardrop-shaped, so begin by drawing this in the center of your paper.

Ⓑ On either side of your teardrop, draw your scorpion's pincers. These are large oval shapes on the end of small arms.

Ⓒ The rest of your scorpion's body is constructed using simple shapes. First of all, its tail extends from the back of the body and has a bulbous oval on top that will eventually be the sting. The legs of your scorpion are in three segments.

Ⓓ You can now draw your scorpion's claw-like pincers and its body armor. The pincers are two joined teardrop shapes, one overlapping the other, and the body armor is made up of many sections. Finally, the sting has a sharp point on the end for piercing and paralyzing its victims!

Ⓔ Start to add detail to the scorpion. Begin sketching in the eyes and some smaller pincers around the mouth area. Overlap each section of the armor on the scorpion's body.

Ⓕ Draw over your lines in black pen and erase any pencil lines. You are now ready to color in your scorpion.

Ⓖ Color your scorpion in your own choice of tones and hues. The one shown here features yellow that blends into black on each plate of armor. Once done, stand back from your page, and look at what you have drawn—it's very scary isn't it?

2

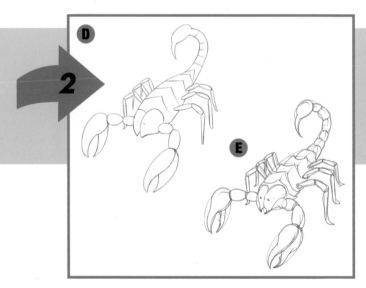

3

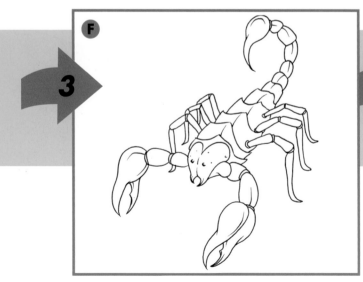

4

HOW TO DRAW A DRAGONFLY

STEP 1

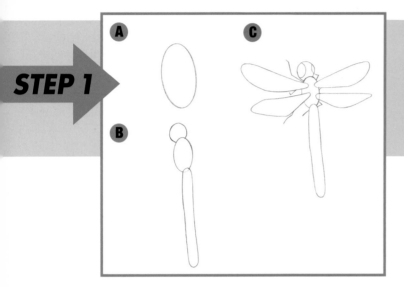

A Begin your dragonfly picture by drawing an oval shape in the center of your page. Remember to draw this at a slight angle. This oval is going to be the thorax of your dragonfly.

B Next, draw a long thin sausage shape directly below the thorax—this will be your dragonfly's abdomen. Now draw its head, a small circular shape sitting on top of the thorax.

C The dragonfly is going to need some legs and wings. The legs are simple sticks, and the wings are like large sails. It also has large, round, faceted eyes on either side of its head.

2

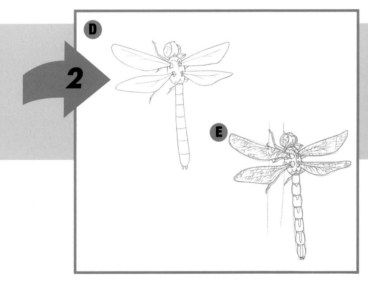

D Start adding the detail to your dragonfly. The wings have veins running down them, and the abdomen has stripes all the way along it. The dragonfly's eyes contain reflections from the sun. You can now fatten the legs a little.

E The dragonfly's wings are broken down into lots of patterned compartments, and you can place these quite randomly. The stripes on the abdomen are given extra detail down the center, and it has furry patches where the wings meet the thorax.

F When your dragonfly is looking the way you want it to, draw in the outline using a black pen, and erase the pencil marks.

G Insects look great painted in strong primary colors, so the dragonfly should be predominantly yellow, with green eyes and brown details. Blue or red would look just as good, though.

3

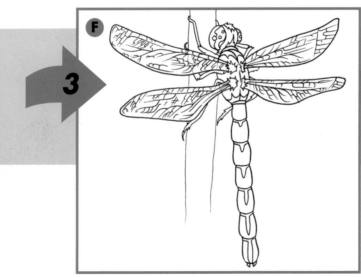

4

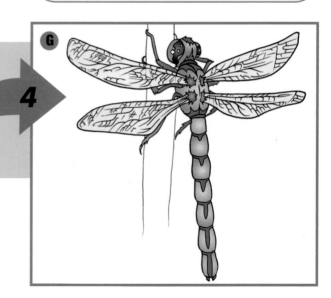

STEP 1

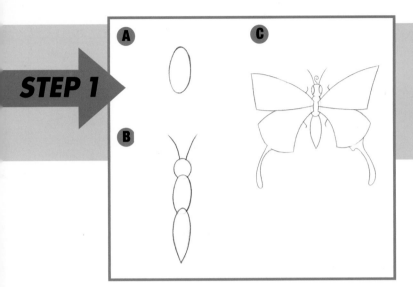

2

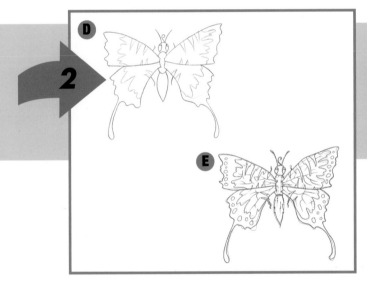

A Start your butterfly by drawing a small thin oval in the center of your paper. This is going to be the thorax for your butterfly.

B The other two parts of the butterfly's body are called the head and the abdomen. The head sits on top of the thorax, and is a small circle with two antennae on top. The abdomen is like an upside down teardrop, and is drawn under the thorax.

C To fly, your butterfly needs wings that are almost triangular in shape. The lower wings have "tails" hanging down from them that look like a trail of liquid paint. Next, draw eyes on either side of the head and a curled tongue on top.

D The details of butterfly are mainly on the wings, which can have fantastic patterns covering them. Remember the one important rule: keep it symmetrical—whatever you draw on one wing should be exactly mirrored on the other.

E Draw some final details on your butterfly's wings and make its body look "fuzzy" all over. You can now add some reflections in its eyes.

F Draw over your pencil sketch with a black pen in order to create your final outline. Then erase the pencil, and your butterfly is ready to color in.

G Any color goes with the butterfly but to make a real impact on the page, stick with "the brighter, the better" rule. The one shown here is actually a butterfly called a "Red Admiral," that is black and orange.

3

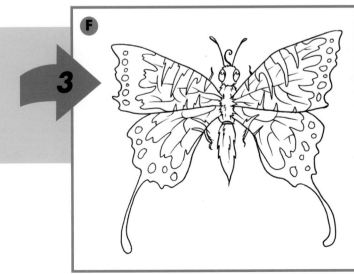

4

HOW TO DRAW A FISH

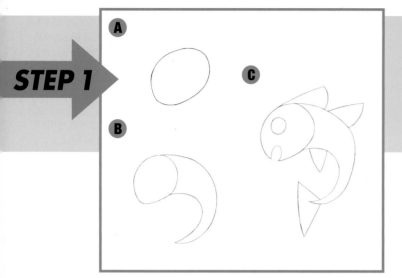

A A fish's head is shaped like a large egg. Start by drawing this shape in the center of your paper.

B The second stage is to draw the fish's tail, which is shaped like a large curved horn and is attached to the head.

C Your fish needs some fins to swim with! Make these from fan shapes. One is placed behind the head, two are placed on the sides, and a final fan shape makes up the tail. Draw a circular eye on the head, as well as an oval-shaped mouth cut into the outline of the head.

D Now you can start adding some simple detail to the fish's frame. Give it three thin gills behind its head, another eye bulging from the side of its head, and make sure the fan-shaped fins now have sharp edges. This fish also has curved spikes on the end of its tail, a rubbery mouth, and splashes of water around its body.

E You should create some texture on the fish's skin. Many fish have scales covering the skin, and you can create this effect by drawing small "C" shapes all along body. Next, add details to the glassy eyes. Finally, put some finishing touches to the fins.

F Once you're happy with how your fish looks, you can draw over the lines in black pen, before erasing the original pencil lines.

G Fish come in a wide variety of colors, but for a three-dimensional look, shade from one color to another like in the picture here.

2

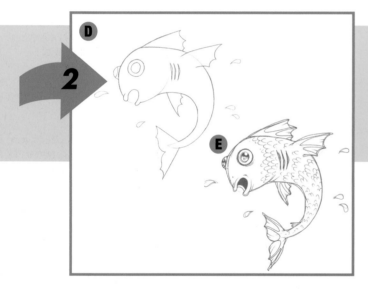

3

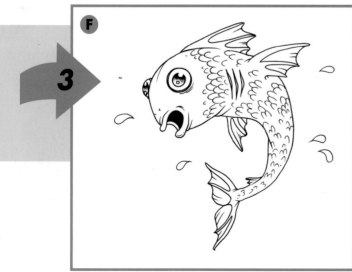

4

STEP 1

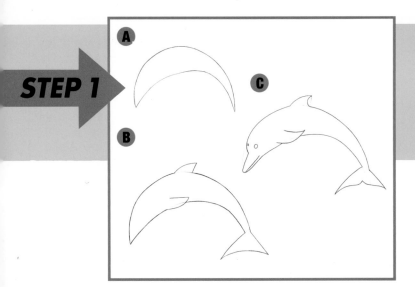

2

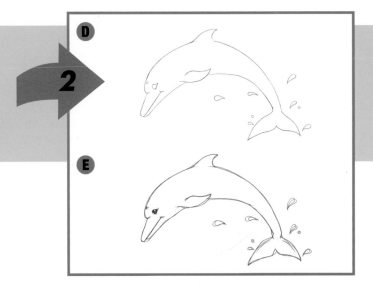

A Draw a large crescent moon shape on your page, with the pointed edges facing downward. This shape is the basic form of your dolphin.

B Your dolphin has fins shaped like a triangle with one curved edge, like a quarter of a circle. The tail is a larger triangle with a curved bottom edge.

C The shape of your dolphin's face is created by cutting into your crescent shape and giving it a curved snout and rounded forehead. Its face consists of a small eye, a smiling mouth, and a single "nostril" on the forehead. You should also give the top fin and tail a curvier look, using your pencil.

D After the dolphin's framework is finished, start adding some simple detail. The eye will look a lot friendlier if you give it a more fan-shaped eyelid. Draw splashes of water to make it look like the dolphin is leaping out of the ocean.

E Sketch detail onto your dolphin, such as wrinkles where the flippers meet the body, and a glint of light in the eye.

F Before adding any color to your dolphin, trace over your pencil version in black pen and erase the pencil lines. This will prevent any smudging of the outline when you add color.

G You can now color in your dolphin using gray tones. To achieve the best effect, shade gradually from a darker gray on top to a light gray on the underside.

3

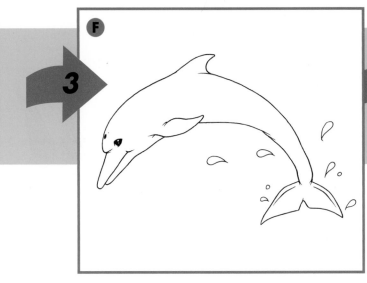

4

HOW TO DRAW A SHARK

STEP 1

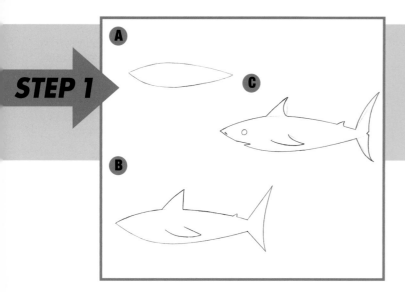

2

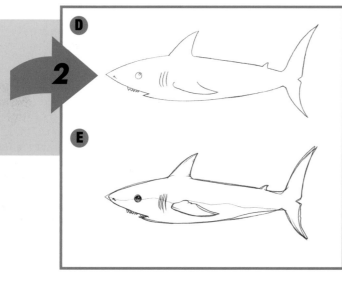

3

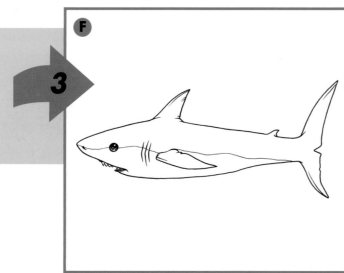

4

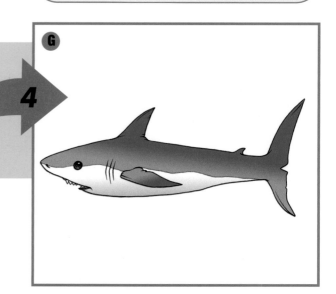

A Sketch a long almond shape in the center of the page—this is going to be your shark's body. The front edge of this is a little fatter than the back.

B Draw a curved triangular shape on top of the body to represent its main fin. The other fins are similar in shapes, and the tail is a large triangle with a curved section at the rear. Make the tail longer at the top than at the bottom.

C Your shark's face is constructed using simple shapes. Its mouth is a triangular shape cut into the main body, and the eye is a circle. Start to give the fins a more curved appearance, and scoop a small triangle from the tail.

D The shark's gills are drawn using three simple curved lines. Draw a row of sharp triangular teeth in its mouth and put a small circular reflection in the eye. Also start rounding off the edges where the fins and tail meet the body.

E Now alter anything you aren't happy with before sketching a faint wobbly line about halfway down the body from nose to tail. Great White sharks in particular have undersides that are much paler than the rest of their bodies, so this line will help separate that lighter underbelly from the dark upper body.

F Draw over the pencil lines that you want to use with a black drawing pen and erase any leftover pencil lines.

G Your man-eater is now ready to color! The shark here features a turquoise-gray combination.

STEP 1

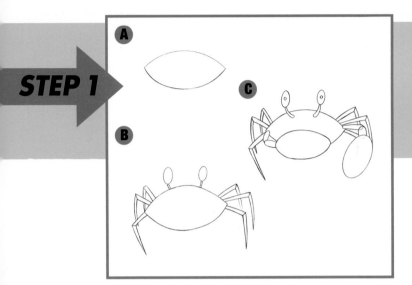

A Your crab begins life as a large almond shape. This is going to be its body, so it needs to be quite large and placed in the center of the paper.

B The legs of your crab consist of two sections, the lower one tapering to a point. Two fairly small ovals are joined to the body with stalks—these are your crab's eyes.

C Now your crab needs some arms. These are created using one oval as the upper arm, and another for the forearm. These are connected to the body at either side. Finally, it needs huge pincers on the end of each arm to fight enemies and catch food!

2

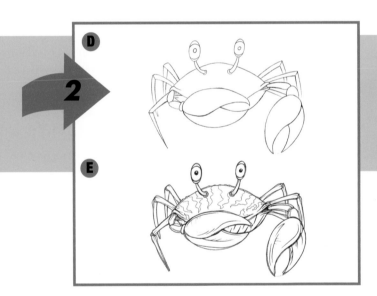

D Your crab is almost done, except for the final shape of the pincers. These claws are the sharp, curved shapes at the end of the arms. To draw these, split each oval into sharp, "teardrop" shapes. Next, give the eyelids and pupils some detail.

E Now add details to the crab's tough shell, such as stripes running along the top, and lines along the joints of the legs to give them a bony look.

F Once your crab is looking suitably "armored," you can draw over the pencil lines with a black pen, and erase any pencil lines that aren't needed.

G To complete your picture of the crab, it's time to color it in using colored pencils, felt-tip pens, pastels, or paints.

3

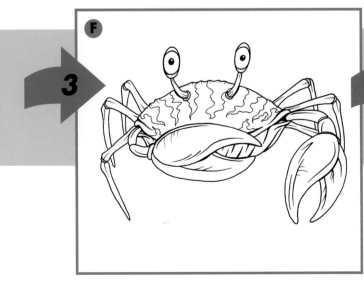

4

STEP 1

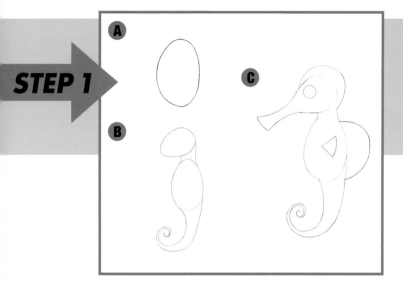

A The first stage of your seahorse drawing will look like a giant oval or "egg" shape—this is the seahorse's body.

B Draw another egg shape on top of the first, joined by a short neck. Next, add your seahorse's tail, a long, coiled horn shape.

C Give your seahorse a thin, trumpet-shaped snout, a circular eye, and a semi-circular crest on the head. The fin starts off as a triangular "fan" shape, and it has a large semi-circular "sail" on its back.

D Start adding simple detail to your seahorse, such as spiked edges on the crest and "sail," a frilled edge to the fin, and a tiny pupil in his eye. You can also begin sketching in some seaweed floating in the water beside it.

2

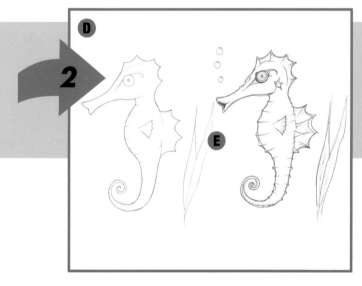

E Next, add the final touches to the face by adding lines in the eyes that branch out from the pupil. Give it a tiny fin, similar to the spiked crest, behind the head. Make the entire body outline look spiny by drawing lines down it, and joining these with the scooped lines. Finally, draw round bubbles coming out of its snout.

F Use a black pen to draw over your design before erasing the pencil lines.

G Seahorses are quite often sand-colored, so they can blend in with their surroundings and avoid predators. Use a few similar tones of color, and blend from one to the other to help your seahorse hide from hungry enemies!

3

4

STEP 1

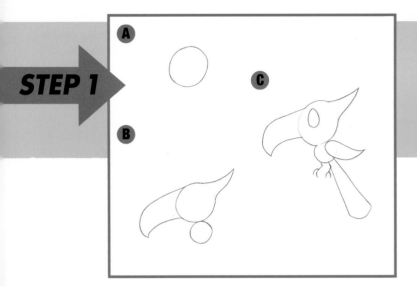

A The first shape you should draw on your page to create a parrot is a large circle. You don't have to be exact with this, as it is just the basic starting shape for your parrot's head.

B Draw a large beak on the left of the circle and a bent triangular shape on the right, to form your parrot's head. Next, draw a circle about half the size and below the first one to represent the parrot's body. Being a cartoon parrot means that it can get away with having a huge head, yet still fly!

C The parrot has tiny stick-like feet and a tear-drop-shaped wing. Its tail is a long fan shape, and the eyes start off by being egg-shaped.

2

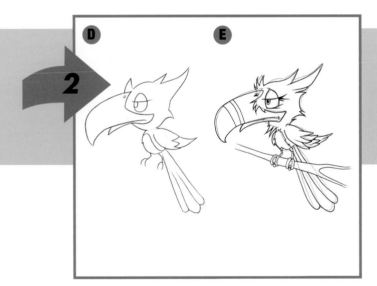

D Now, sketch a few details onto your bird. It has a dumb-looking face, with half-open eyes and a head of ruffled feathers. The nostrils sit at the top of the beak, near the eyes. Separate the tail into three large feathers, and the wing into sections.

E To add to the realism of your character, layer the feathers over each other and draw some smaller, fluffy feathers around the beak. Draw lashes on the eyes if you want your parrot to look female, but if you want a boy parrot, leave these off. Finally, fatten the stick-like legs a little and draw the perch it's sitting on.

F Draw over the character with a thin black pen, before you erase the pencil lines.

G You can use pencils or paints to complete your character.

3

4

HOW TO DRAW A PENGUIN

STEP 1

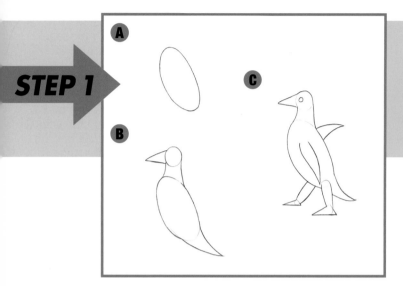

A For the penguin, draw a large oval in the center of your page, roughly twice as long as it is high, but don't worry about being exact. Draw this shape at an angle, as if it were falling over.

B Using the first shape as a guide, draw a small circle, joined by two lines, to the top of the large oval, and add a long triangular beak. The tail is a triangle that curves slightly upward.

C Draw two wings on your penguin—these resemble flippers, so they should be sleek and smooth. Next, draw your penguin's legs. These are thin oval shapes with triangles for feet. The left leg is slightly hidden behind the body.

D To complete the basic frame for your penguin, join all of your shapes together with a smooth outline. Draw its tiny, beady eye with a white ring behind it, and sketch a line down the body to separate the black top feathers from the white underside. Finally, give the legs some fluffy feathers and his feet curved toenails.

2

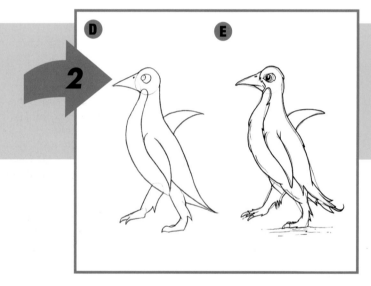

E Time to add those finishing touches—the most important thing is to make the penguin look like it has feathers, but not fluffy ones. Penguins have smooth, oily feathers to help them survive in Antarctic conditions.

F Draw over your penguin with a drawing pen. Wait a few minutes for the ink to dry, then erase any remaining pencil lines.

G Color your penguin using either felt-tip pen or colored pencils.

3

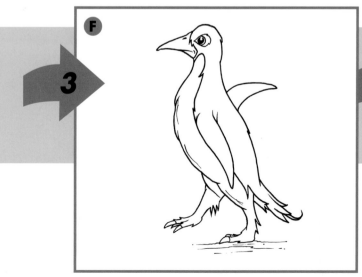

4

STEP 1

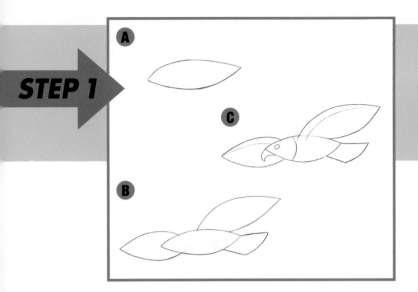

2

3

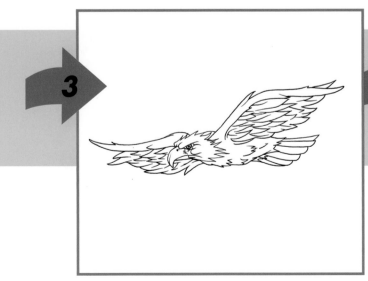

4

A Start your eagle by sketching a faint leaf shape on your paper. This is its body.

B The eagle's wings are a similar shape, but one wing overlaps the head slightly, so be careful with your pencil and don't press too hard. The tail is a simple fan shape.

C Your eagle's legs are tucked away while it flies, so you won't have to draw them. Draw a large hooked beak on the front of the head, an oval-shaped eye, and a collar where the white head feathers will begin on the neck.

D Start to add simple detail to your eagle. The sharp piercing eyes have small pupils that help it spot its prey, and the beak has a tiny nostril on the top. Start to draw the feathers by using jagged pencil lines around the "collar" and down the edge of the wings. Finally, the fan-shaped tail is split into five separate feathers.

E Final details can now be applied to your eagle such as sharp wispy feathers along the inside of the wings and a frowning face. Draw lots of curvy, jagged lines around the face to make it look like as if the ruffled feathers are being blown by the wind as the bird flies along.

F It's time to trace over the lines you've drawn with a black pen, and don't forget to erase any leftover pencil lines.

G Give the body feathers a deep, warm brown tone, leaving the face feathers white. The eyes are yellow, as is the powerful, curved beak.

HOW TO DRAW A DOG

STEP 1

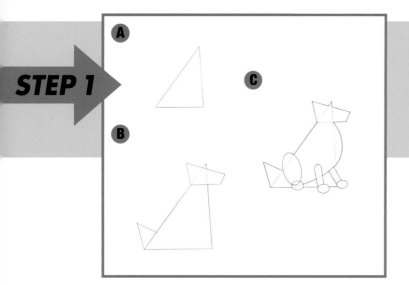

A Start your picture by drawing a tall, right-angled triangle in the center of your paper. This is going to be the main body of your dog.

B Now draw the head, which is also triangular, but with one of the corners cut off. Make this shape overlap the first triangle. Then draw a much smaller triangle near the base of the original triangle. This will be your dog's tail.

C Give your dog a rounded chest. Next, add the cylindrical front legs and the oval feet. Because the back legs are tucked in underneath this dog, you can only see one of them, and it needs to be oval-shaped.

D It's time for those details! Add simple facial features and start rounding off the sharp edges. Draw three separate toes on each of the dog's paws, and give it a wet nose and a lolling tongue. Finally, start to draw the fur. Begin by drawing lines that wrap around the body.

E Draw some final detail on your dog. The fur is separated into large sections, each of these sections can be a different color. Give the fur a shaggy appearance by using short, sharp strokes with your pencil.

F Draw over your sketch with a black pen. Then erase the pencil, and the dog is ready to color.

G This dog is a rough-coated Collie, so it should be colored in sandy browns, grays, and white. Color the tongue a fleshy pink and make the eye dark brown.

2

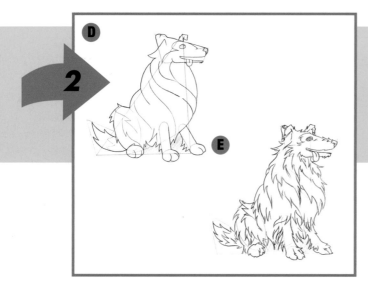

3

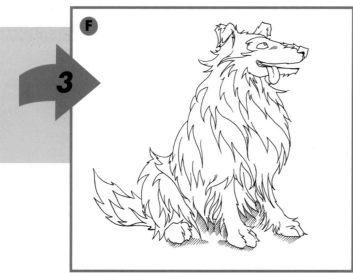

4

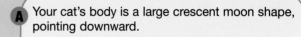

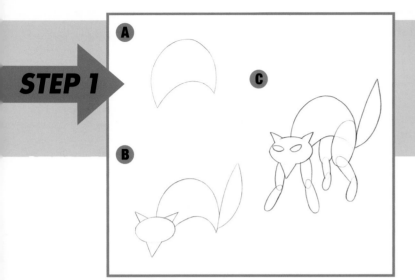

STEP 1

A Your cat's body is a large crescent moon shape, pointing downward.

B The head of your cat is an oval with two triangular ears and a triangle that will form its open mouth. It has an almond-shaped tail that it is waving in the air.

C The cat's legs are constructed using oval shapes. The front legs consist of two ovals, and the hind legs consist of three. Notice how the legs bend backward on a cat, unlike the human leg that bends forward from the knee. Once you've drawn the legs, give your cat two narrow, slanting eyes.

D Using the frame as a guide, start to add detail to your cat. Begin sketching the fur, which is jagged and standing on end. This cat isn't too happy! Next, give it three toes on each foot and start to sketch in an angry mouth.

E Your cat will need some sharp teeth and whiskers. It is hissing at a dog, so the mouth is wide open and the tongue is showing. Finally, give your cat white "socks" on the feet.

F Draw over your picture with a black drawing pen or narrow felt-tip pen. Once you have gone over all of the lines, erase the leftover pencil lines.

G Cats are usually black, white, ginger, or calico, so it's best to stick with these colors. This cat has bright green eyes to make it look mad, but maybe your cat could be a little more laid back? Experiment with different colors!

2

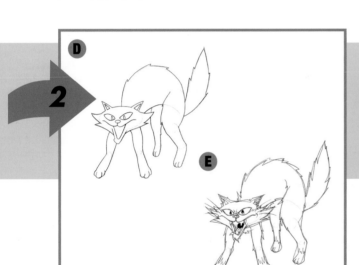

3

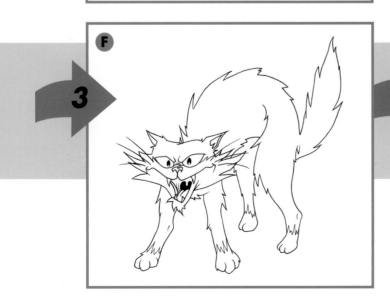

4

HOW TO DRAW A RABBIT

STEP 1

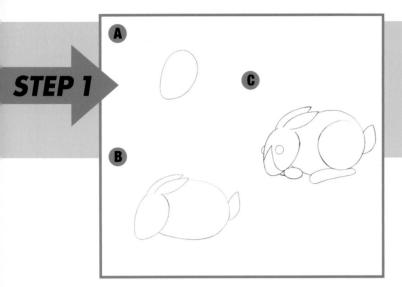

2

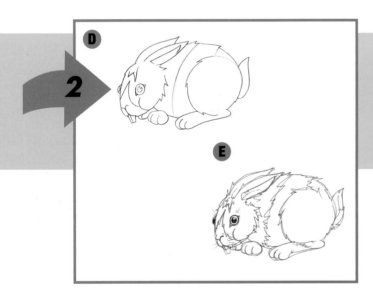

A To begin your picture, draw an oval shape for the rabbit's head.

B Draw two large ears on top of your oval. Then, slightly overlapping the head shape, draw a much larger oval for the rabbit's body. Finally, give your rabbit a little cotton-bud tail.

C To complete your rabbit's basic frame, it will need legs. The hind leg is quite large, and consists of a circle with a rounded cylindrical shape underneath. The front feet are oval shapes, tucked under the head. Next, give it two round eyes and a triangular stripe on the nose.

D Start adding simple details to your rabbit, such as the teeth and nostrils. Add some detail to the eyes, such as the pupils and a reflection. Use jagged lines when drawing the outline of your rabbit, as this will make it look furry.

E Add some final detail to your rabbit. Keep sketching jagged lines all over its body to give it that fluffy appearance, and separate the feet, drawing three toes on each of them.

F Before coloring your rabbit, draw over the pencil lines with a black pen, remembering not to trace over any lines that you don't want.

G You can color your rabbit in various ways. You can get excellent results with paints or colored pencils, which will make your rabbit picture really come to life.

3

4

STEP 1

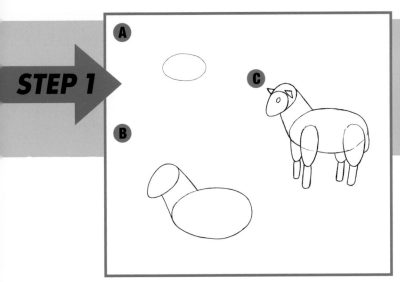

Ⓐ Draw a large horizontal oval shape in the center of your paper to create the sheep's body.

Ⓑ On the top of your oval shape, draw an egg shape connected to the oval by a wide collar. This should now look like a head and neck attached to the sheep's body.

Ⓒ Give your sheep some legs to walk on. The tops of these are oval, with lower-leg "stick" shapes underneath. You should also add detail to your sheep's face, such as an oval eye and some pointed ears. Next, draw a short tail.

Ⓓ Draw some hooves on your character and make the face a little shapelier. Finally, you can stick a clump of grass in its mouth. Sheep are grazing animals, so it's rare not to see one chewing!

2

Ⓔ Your sheep is almost finished, but the fleece needs to be a lot fluffier: a little like cotton candy in fact. Add the "fluff" as if you are drawing a cloud, making lots of tiny curved lines. Give your sheep some pupils in the eye and some flared nostrils.

Ⓕ Use a black pen to fill in the outline, and erase those pencil lines. You're now ready to start coloring in.

Ⓖ Of course, it's best to use black and white for your sheep—after all, how often have you seen a purple sheep? Or an orange one? But, if you want to experiment with different colors, then don't let reality stop you—go for it! You may surprise yourself with the results.

3

4

HOW TO DRAW A PIG

STEP 1

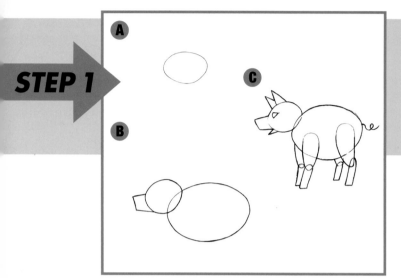

A Your pig's body is oval shaped and should be drawn fairly large in the center of your page.

B Like the body, this pig's head is oval but smaller of course. Set the head at the same angle as the body, and slightly overlapping, but make the shape a little fatter and rounder. Next, give the pig a short, boxy snout.

C Draw your pig's legs using simple shapes. The hind legs bend back at the knee, and are a touch bigger than the front legs. The feet are flat and quite narrow. It has a triangular bottom lip and large triangular ears. Don't forget the thin, curly tail!

D Start to pencil in your pig's facial features, such as the nostrils and half-open eye. Next, curve the ears a little and begin to give the feet some shape.

E The important final details on your pig are the face and skin. It has a very wrinkly snout and reflective eyes. The skin creases where the limbs meet the body, and the legs are quite thin and bony, in contrast to the fat, round body.

F Trace over your drawing using a black drawing pen. Then you can erase the pencil lines. Your porky pig or hog is now ready to color.

G You should ideally color your pig either pink or black, or a combination of the two. Or, if you're feeling daring, make it any color you want—experiment and see what happens!

2

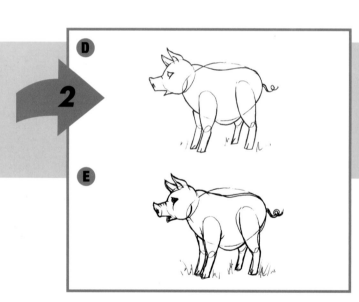

3

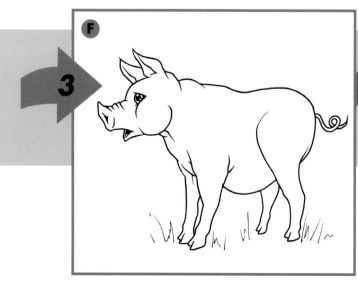

4

STEP 1

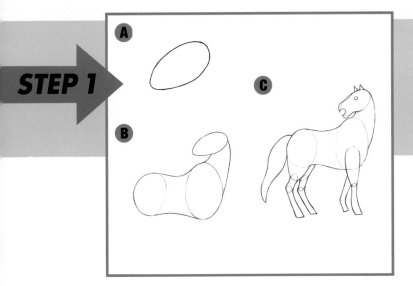

A The horse's head is shaped like an egg. Start by drawing this shape on the right-hand side of your paper, with the pointed part of the egg facing slightly downward.

B The horse's body consists of two large oval shapes, joined together by two dipping lines. The front oval is twice as long as the horse's head, while the back oval is about the same length, but a little fatter. Join this body shape to the head by drawing a thick neck.

C Draw your horse's back legs with three simple shapes—a large oval, a much smaller oval, and a stick shape. Its front legs consist of an oval and a stick shape. Give your horse a thick tail and then start to shape the face a little. The bridge of the nose should narrow slightly before widening again toward the mouth. It has triangular ears and an oval eye.

2

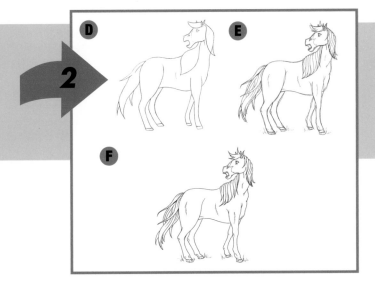

D Draw the outline of your horse by joining all the body shapes together with flowing lines. Now begin to add detail like the horse's mane and the white stripe on the end of its nose. Draw some extra spiky shapes on the tail so that it appears to be blowing in the wind.

E Use heavier pencil lines to give the eye long, pointed eyelashes and a reflection. The nostrils should flare, to look as if it is whinnying. Final touches to the legs, such as the hooves and bony knees, give the horse a more realistic look. The mane and tail are segmented into clumps of hair so that they give the impression of real movement.

F It's time to draw over the lines in black pen, before erasing the original pencil lines.

3

G This horse has a brown coat with a white flash on its nose, but horses can be white, black, or mottled. You can use colored pencils, paints or pastels to color in your picture. Perhaps, though, you have your very own horse? If so, you could use these tips to draw your own horse, color it in, and then pin the finished picture up in your horse's stable. Now there's an idea!

STEP 1

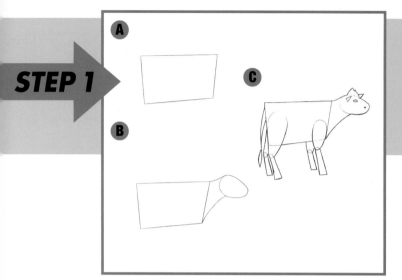

2

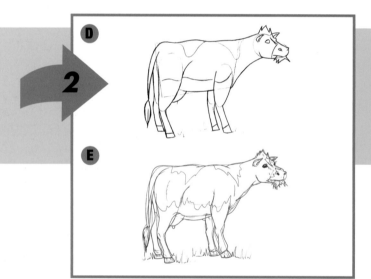

A Like all cows, the one featured here is quite a box-shaped character, so the first shape you should draw on your page is a large, irregular oblong.

B Draw an egg shape to form your cow's head. This is joined to the boxy body by making two curved lines to form a neck.

C All of the cow's legs are drawn with two shapes: an oval (which is larger on the hind legs) and a thin stick-like shape beneath them. Now, start to work on the face: she will have pointed ears and a fluffy patch of hair. She doesn't have any horns, though.

D Start to round off any sharp corners on your cow's body. Cows may be box-shaped, but there aren't any sharp corners on a real cow! The egg-shaped head should be narrower along the nose and she should have large, calm eyes. Sketch some grass in her mouth, and don't forget her udders: a simple cup shape.

E The pattern on the cow's fur helps to determine what breed of cow she is. Being a Friesian cow, this one has patches of white on her back, plus a white underside. She has sturdy, yet bony legs.

F Draw over the character with a thin black pen, before you erase the remaining pencil lines.

G It's time to finish your cow drawing—use pencils, paints or pastels to color in your cow. Don't forget to give her a name!

3

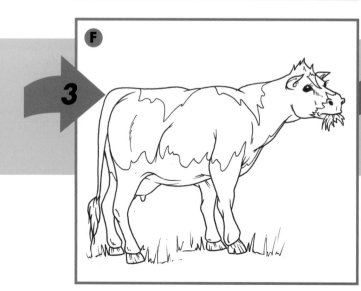

4

STEP 1

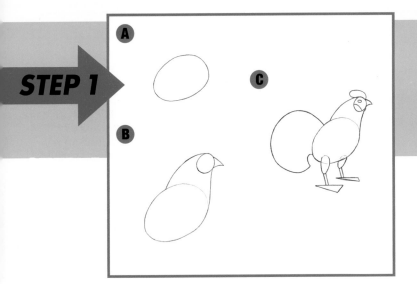

A The main body of the rooster is an oval, which you should draw at an angle in the center of your page.

B Draw a small circle that has two sweeping curved lines that join at the bottom of the circle and add a short, stumpy, triangular beak.

C Draw a large curved tail on your rooster. Next, draw his legs. These are thin oval shapes with stick-shaped lower legs and triangles for feet. The rooster has an oval eye and a simple crest shaped a little like a baked bean.

D To complete the basic frame of your rooster, start to sketch some fluffy feathers along the base of his tail and give his feet three toes, each with curved claws. The feathers on the rooster's chest start as curved lines that follow the contour of his body. You should also sketch the shape of the wing down the side of the body.

2

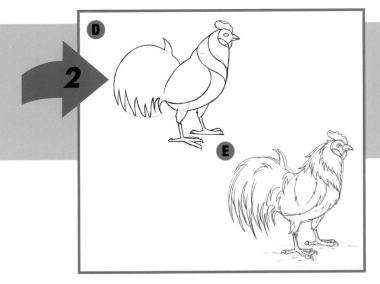

E When detailing, it is important to make your rooster look like he has lots of ruffled feathers! These are drawn using sweeping strokes for the large feathers and shorter jagged strokes for the small ones. Finally, his feet have tiny wrinkles all the way down them, and he has beady eyes.

F Draw over your rooster with a pen, and wait a few minutes for the ink to dry before erasing any remaining pencil lines.

G The final stage of your bird is adding color. Consider using watercolors because they are a great way to blend the colors on his tail and wing.

3

4

HOW TO DRAW A LION

STEP 1

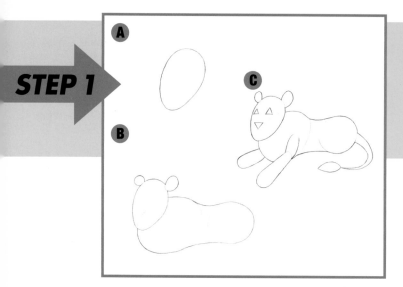

A First, draw an upturned egg shape for your lion's head. This should be fairly large, but remember that you'll need to fit his body on one side of it, so draw it on the left of the page.

B Draw a larger, longer egg under the first and overlap it slightly. This shape is going to be the front part of your lion's body. Then draw an egg about the same size as the head, joined to the front of his body by two dipped lines. The overall body shape should look like a footprint. Next, give your lion two small oval ears.

C Draw in his front legs and tail. The legs are created using simple shapes—the right leg is made out of two shapes, while the left leg is a single oval, hidden behind the lion's chest. His tail is long and thin with a tasselled tip, and his eyes and nose are triangles.

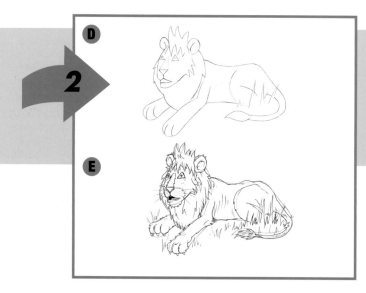

D Now add his face and his large shaggy mane. Draw three toes on each foot, and the crease of the back leg that is bent under him in the grass.

E Draw in his long whiskers, spiky fringe, and the stripe down his nose. The paws have claws protruding from them, and the ribs show slightly through the body fur.

F Before coloring your lion, draw over your pencil lines with a black pen.

G Lions are a yellow color with a darker mane. The eyes would normally be yellow too, but as this is a cartoon, he has more human-looking white eyes to add character.

STEP 1

2

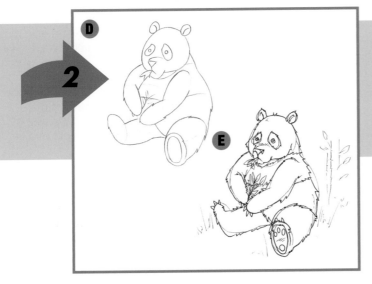

A Start your drawing with a slightly squashed circle. This is actually the beginning of your panda's head.

B Now draw a larger, overlapping circular shape beneath the head, before giving the head two small round ears.

C Complete the panda's body by giving it arms and legs. The right leg is in front, with the bottom of the foot showing. The other leg is stretched out further back, so it is drawn smaller and thinner to create perspective. The arms are each made of two oval shapes, bent at the elbow because the panda will be holding some leaves.

D Now start to give the panda a jagged, furry outline. Begin adding the facial features, such as the sad-looking eyes and the downturned mouth with a leaf in it.

E Add some final touches such as the pads on the bottom of the panda's front foot, and the small claws that help it grip its food. Draw a furry stripe around the body, and the arms and legs.

F Draw over your pencil sketch with a black pen in order to create a final outline. Then erase the pencil.

G Of course, you don't need much coloring for a panda—it's mainly black and white, but little touches, such as brown eyes and the green leaves it's holding and eating, will really stand out and bring the picture to life.

3

4

HOW TO DRAW A GIRAFFE

STEP 1

A Use an egg shape to create the giraffe's body. It needs to be quite large and low down on the paper so you have space for the long neck.

B The giraffe's head is also an oval shape, but it's less than half the size of its body. The head is joined to the body by an incredibly long neck that is thinner near the head, but widens slightly toward the body. Finish the head with two leaf-shaped ears and two little "horns."

C The giraffe's legs are created using oval shapes, with long pole shapes for the lower legs. Remember that the back legs are in three sections and bend backward. It has a thin tail with a tassel on the end.

D Draw your giraffe's outline using the shapes as a guide. Connect the shapes, remembering which are supposed to overlap and which are not. Start sketching in the giraffe's face and give it a thin mane all the way down the neck. Next, give the legs some hooves.

E Now draw creases where the legs join the body. Giraffes have a kind of "jigsaw" pattern of patches on the body. Achieve this by drawing different sized uneven shapes. Be bold and try to vary the size of the pattern.

F You can now draw over the pencil lines with a black pen, and then erase any pencil lines.

G It's time to color in your drawing. Use yellow for the fur and brown for the "jigsaw" patches on the body.

2

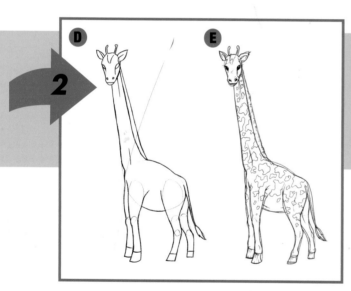

3

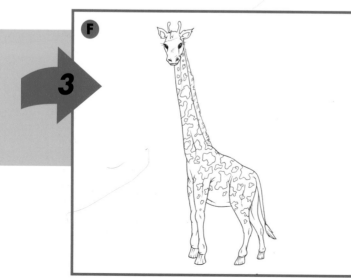

4

STEP 1

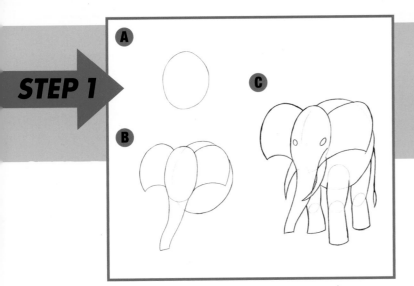

A Draw a large, round shape on the page to create the elephant's body.

B The head of the elephant is about half the size of its body. This oval shape overlaps the elephant's body. On either side of this shape, draw your elephant's ears, which are shaped like big sails. The elephant now needs a trunk. This is simply a long snake-like shape.

C Complete the elephant's frame by giving it some legs, tusks, and a tail. The legs are like tree trunks, but one of the back legs is hidden from view behind the front legs.

D Using the shapes as a guide, connect them using simple, bold lines. The ears are ragged along the bottom edge, and the feet have large, semi-circular toenails.

E Now finalize the elephant's facial features—it has a bald head and small, dark, almond-shaped eyes. Elephants are also quite wrinkly, and have very tough skin. Make the knees look wrinkled by drawing a swirl on each one.

F Now you're ready to trace over the pencil lines you've drawn with a black pen. Don't forget to erase any pencil lines that are left over. With this done, you are now ready to color in the finished drawing.

G Elephants are gray with cream-colored tusks. For the very best results, use colored pencils, which are ideal because they give a grainy appearance.

2

3

4

HOW TO DRAW A SNAKE

STEP 1

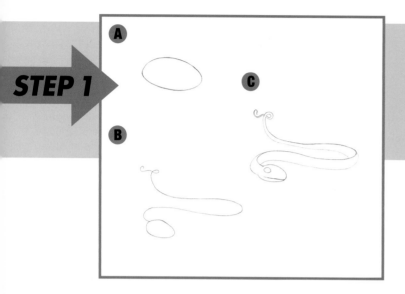

A Begin by drawing the snake's head in the shape of a large egg on your paper. The head should be closer to the bottom of the page, because the snake's body will be curling above its head.

B Draw a long, squiggly line up from the head to create the snake's body.

C The snake's body now needs to be fattened out. The line you drew in the previous step is actually the snake's "spine," so it should rest on the top of his body. Next, draw an almond-shaped eye and a mouth.

D Add some simple detail to your snake's face, such as a long, thin forked tongue and a slit-shaped pupil.

E To enhance the look of the snake's skin, draw triangular stripes down the length of the body. The snake featured here has fairly smooth skin, except for a few wrinkles, but you may want yours to have more scales and maybe a rattle at the tip of the tail.

F Now trace over your pencil lines with a thin black marker or drawing pen. Then you can erase the pencil lines, and your slithery snake is ready to color.

G You can color your snake any way you want to but it's a good idea to use bright colors. Some snakes are bright green, but the one featured is an attractive and eye-grabbing red and yellow. Don't be afraid to experiment and see what you can come up with!

2

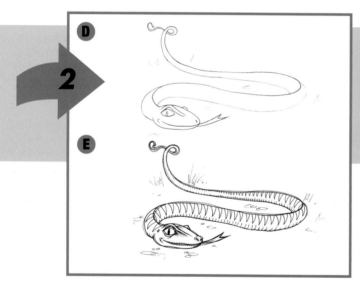

3

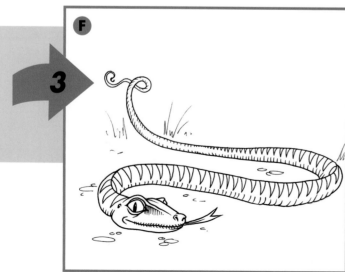

4

STEP 1

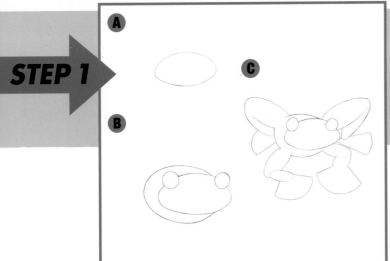

A Start by drawing a large oval shape on the page. This is going to be your frog's head.

B Draw a larger oval behind the head and slightly to the left. Next, draw two circles on top of the head, which are going to be the frog's distinctive, bug-eyes.

C Your frog's legs are made using two oval shapes, and two large fan shapes are used for its feet. The back legs are bent backward and tucked in behind the body.

D Begin adding detail to your frog's face and feet. Give the eyes pupils, and draw a long, thin mouth from one side of the head to the other. The front feet have four toes on each, while the back feet have three.

E Now that you have the basic shape of the frog, you can start to draw the skin. It has striped legs and webbed feet. Pencil in the nostrils and round off the toes. You could also draw a passing fly, that is unaware that it may be the frog's next meal!

F Trace over your picture with a pen, and then erase the original pencil lines. You can now color in your frog using bright shades. Try using watercolor pencils or pastels for the ideal finish. As for the colors themselves, this frog has green skin, but your frog could be red, blue, yellow, or whatever color you want. Remember to experiment!

2

3

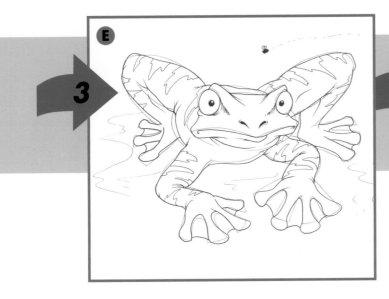

4

STEP 1

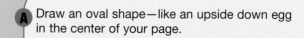

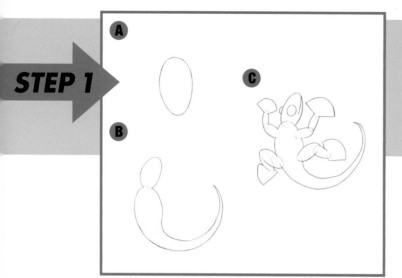

2

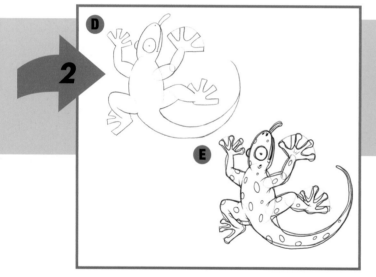

3

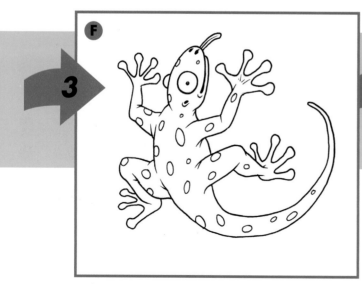

4

A Draw an oval shape—like an upside down egg in the center of your page.

B The gecko's body is an egg shape too, but is much larger. Make this oval overlap the head very slightly, and only lightly pencil in where it crosses the face because you'll need to erase this later. Next, draw a long, horn-shaped tail out of the bottom of the body.

C Your gecko now needs some legs. Draw two long ovals and a fan for each limb, making sure that the upper section is slightly fatter than the lower. Next, draw two large bug-eyes on the head.

D Join all the shapes together to create your gecko's basic outline. Its feet can also be drawn in now, each foot having four toes. Start to sketch its face and remember to give it a very long tongue.

E Begin sketching in some simple detail, such as the spotted skin. Round off the gecko's toes and sketch some wrinkles where the limbs meet its body.

F Now draw over the pencil lines you want to keep, using a fine black pen. Then erase the remaining pencil lines.

G Experiment with different color combinations on a separate piece of paper before coloring in your gecko—you can really go nuts with this one, as geckos are lots of crazy colors in real-life!

STEP 1

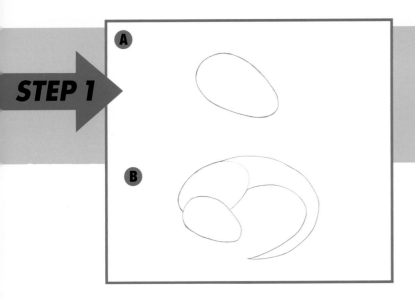

A The crocodile's head is shaped like a large egg, with the more pointed side facing downward. Start by drawing this shape in the center of the paper.

B Now draw the body and tail. The body is a very large egg shape, overlapping the head slightly. The part that overlaps will be hidden behind the head, so don't press too hard! The crocodile's tail is shaped like a large, curved horn.

2

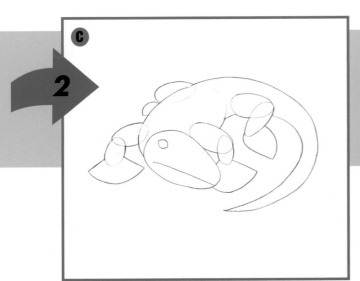

C His legs are constructed using oval shapes for the upper and lower part of the legs, and a fan shape for each foot. Remember that two of his legs are hidden behind his body, so don't be too firm with your pencil because you will need to erase these lines later on.

D Now add simple detail to the crocodile's frame. Give him stubby toes on each foot, and draw in where his eye and mouth are going to be.

E Now add some texture on the crocodile's skin. These creatures have tough scaly skin, and you can create the effect of these scales by using a technique called "cross-hatching." This is when you use overlapping, sketchy diagonal lines. Next, put some folds of skin on his legs and add detail to the face, like some scales round the mouth, and a wrinkled nose. →

3

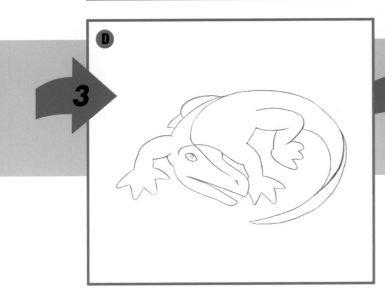

4

5

G

G You can now draw over the lines in black pen, before erasing the original pencil lines.

H This crocodile is colored green to give him a swamp-like look.

6

H